VEGAN MY CHOICE

"Veganism is returning to our roots of compassion."
Rohit Dubey

Copyright © 2024 Rohit
Dubey
All rights reserved

Dedication

My book is dedicated to all vegans like "Acharya Prashant" for being my idol, my muse, and my constant source of inspiration to publish this book.

This book is for those human-beings who care or those who are unaware about the future of planet Earth.

Acknowledgements

As I embark on this journey of sharing the principles and joys of veganism through this book, I'm filled with gratitude and hope. veganism, to me, is not just a dietary choice; it's a way of life that embodies compassion, mindfulness, and sustainability.
Rohit Dubey

Contents

Chapter Name	Page no.
Chapter 1. Introduction	1
Chapter 2. History of Veganism	16
Chapter 3. Earth in 21st Century	33
Chapter 4. To Save our Planet	49
Chapter 5. Foundation of Vegan Lifestyle	59
Chapter 6. Animal Consumption	68
Chapter 7. Impact of Veganism on	80

Chapter 8. Debunking Myths	89
Chapter 9. Health Benefits of Vegan Plate	100
Chapter 10. Practical tips for Vegan Living	109
Chapter 11. Vegan Dairy	119

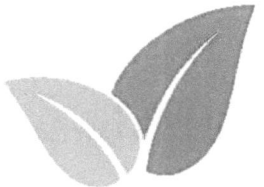

Chapter 1.

INTRODUCTION

I will begin with a beautiful story of compassion and understanding between two very different creatures! It speaks to the power of empathy and kindness, even in the face of danger and adversity. The cow's love for her calf and her willingness to return to the forest, despite the risk, shows the strength of a mother's bond and the importance of family. The tiger's decision to spare the cow's

life and offer protection reflects a deep respect for life and an acknowledgment of the cow's bravery and honesty. In the end, both the cow and the tiger find common ground and form an unlikely friendship, demonstrating that empathy and compassion can bridge even the widest divides. It's a heart-warming reminder that kindness and understanding can truly change the world for its betterment Hello to all readers. First of all, thank you for reading this book. I was born and brought up in a middle-class family in India. Growing up in this rich cultural and spiritual tradition has profoundly shaped my values, beliefs, and way of life. In my family, Here, in India religion is more than just a religion; it is a way Festivals and Celebrations:

Celebrating festivals like **Diwali, Holi, Navaratri and Janmashtami** was always a joyous occasion. These festivals not only brought our family and community together but also reinforced the

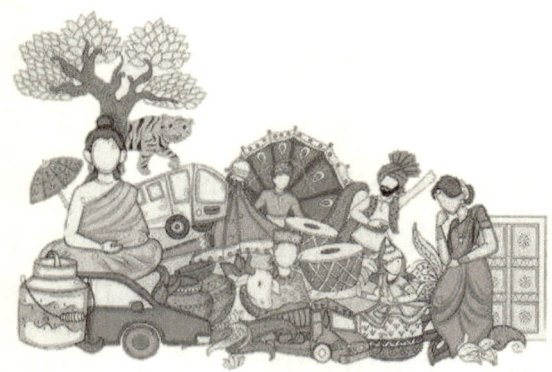

stories and teachings from our sacred texts. Through these celebrations, I learned the significance of family, gratitude, and the triumph of good over evil

From the epics of the Mahabharata and Ramayana to the teachings of the Bhagavad Gita, the stories and scriptures of Hinduism have been a source of inspiration and guidance. These texts taught me valuable life lessons and provided a moral framework that I strive to follow.

Cultural Heritage:

Being part of a family also meant being immersed in a rich cultural heritage. This included classical music and dance, traditional art forms, and a diverse culinary tradition. Each aspect of our culture added a layer of depth to my understanding of the world and my place in it.

Living in my family has been a deeply enriching experience. It has provided me with a strong foundation of spiritual and ethical values, a sense of belonging to a vibrant cultural heritage, and a compassionate outlook towards life. These principles continued to guide me and shape my journey in life.

Cow in Hinduism:

Cows hold a special place in Hinduism, revered for their association with various deities, their role in agricultural life, and their symbolic significance. Cows are seen as a symbol of life and sustenance. They provide essential products such as milk, butter, and ghee, which are vital in the diet and religious practices of Hindus.

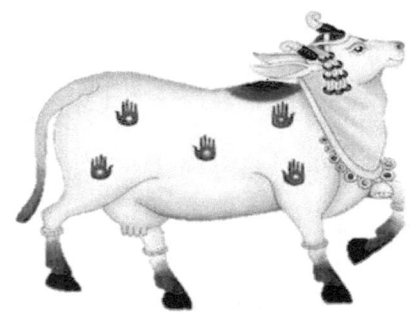

Association with Deities:

Krishna: Lord Krishna, one of the most beloved deities in Hinduism, is often depicted as a cowherd, emphasizing the cow's importance in rural and spiritual life.

Shiva: Nandi, the bull, is the vehicle (vahana) of Lord Shiva, showing the animal's close association with one of the principal deities.

Lakshmi: The cow is sometimes associated with the goddess of wealth, Lakshmi, symbolizing abundance and good fortune.

Kamadhenu: The celestial cow Kamadhenu is considered the mother of all cows and is believed to grant all desires, further elevating the cow's status as sacred.

India has historically been an agricultural nation, and in traditional rural living, cows are necessary for field preparation, dairy production, and even fuel production (dried cow dung). This financial reliance results in a great regard for the animal.

Rituals and Festivals:

Gopastami: A festival dedicated to honoring cows and their caretakers, highlighting their significance in agrarian life.

Gau Puja: Specific rituals like Gau Puja (worship of the cow) involve decorating and worshiping cows, seeking their blessings for prosperity and happiness.

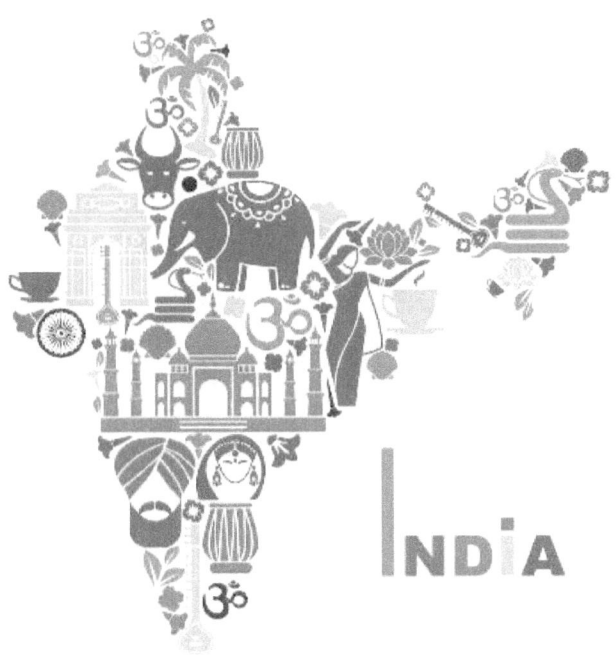

Ethical and Philosophical Views:

Ahimsa (Non-violence): Hinduism emphasizes the principle of ahimsa, or non-violence. This extends to animals, especially cows, and promotes their protection and care.

Symbol of Non-violence and Compassion: The cow represents non-violence and compassion, embodying the principle of ahimsa in its gentleness and nurturing nature.

Historical and Scriptural References:

Vedas and Scriptures: Ancient texts like the Vedas, the Mahabharata, and the Ramayana contain numerous references to cows, underscoring their revered status. The Rigveda, one of the oldest texts, refers to cows as **"Aghnya"** (not to be killed).

Modern Context

Protection Laws:

In contemporary India, many states have laws protecting cows, prohibiting their slaughter, and emphasizing their cultural and religious significance.

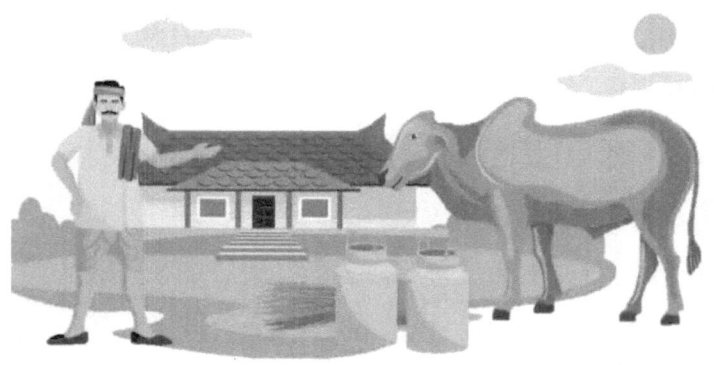

Goshalas: Cow shelters, known as goshalas, are established to care for old and unproductive cows, reflecting continued reverence and care for these animals.

The love for cows in Hinduism is deeply rooted in religious, cultural, and ethical traditions. Cows are revered not only for their practical contributions to daily life but also for the association with deities and their embodiment of non-violence and compassion. This reverence continues to manifest in various rituals, festivals, and protective measures in modern Hindu society.

CHAPTER 2.

HISTORY OF VEGANISM:

The history of veganism is rich and varied, tracing its roots through ancient philosophies, religious practices, and modern ethical movements. Here's a detailed look at the evolution of veganism:

Ancient India and Greece:

India:

Vegetarianism has ancient roots in India, particularly among followers of Jainism, Hinduism, and Buddhism. The principle of ahimsa, or non-violence, is central to these religions, advocating for the avoidance of harm to all living beings, which naturally extended to dietary practices.

Greece:
In ancient Greece, philosophers like Pythagoras promoted a meatless diet for ethical and health reasons. The Pythagorean diet avoided meat and is considered an early form of vegetarianism.

EVOLUTION OF VEGANISM:

Early Modern Period 17th to 19th Century

Enlightenment Era:
In the **17th and 18th** centuries, the Enlightenment period brought renewed interest in animal welfare and ethics. Thinkers like John Locke and Jean-Jacques Rousseau wrote about the moral consideration of animals.

Vegetarian Societies: The modern vegetarian movement began in the early **19th century**. The first Vegetarian Society was founded in England in 1847, and similar societies soon appeared in the United States and Europe.

Birth of veganism mid-20th century:

The term "**vegan**" was coined by **Donald Watson in 1944**. He and a group of non-dairy vegetarians formed the Vegan Society in England to distinguish between those who avoid all animal products and those who consume dairy and eggs. Watson defined veganism as a way of living that seeks to exclude all forms of exploitation of, and cruelty to, animals.

Post War Era 1950s to 1970s:
Health Movements:

The 1950s and 60s saw an increasing focus on the health benefits of plant-based diets. Figures like Dr. John McDougall and Nathan Pritikin advocated for vegetarian and vegan diets to prevent chronic diseases.

Environmental Awareness:

The environmental movement, sparked by Rachel Carson's "Silent Spring"(1962), raised awareness about the ecological impact of industrial practices, including animal agriculture.

Rise of the Animal Rights Movement from 1970s to 1990s:

Peter Singer and Animal Liberation: Peter Singer's book "Animal Liberation" (1975) played a pivotal role in the animal rights movement.

Singer argued for the ethical consideration of animals, promoting veganism as a moral choice.

Grassroots Activism: During the 1980s and 90s, animal rights activism grew, with organizations like PETA (People for the Ethical Treatment of Animals) campaigning against animal cruelty and promoting veganism.

21st Century Mainstream Acceptance 2000's to Present:

Social Media and Celebrities: The rise of social media platforms and endorsements from celebrities like Ellen DeGeneres, Beyoncé, and Joaquin Phoenix have popularized veganism. Documentaries such as "Forks Over Knives" (2011), "Cowspiracy" (2014), and "What the

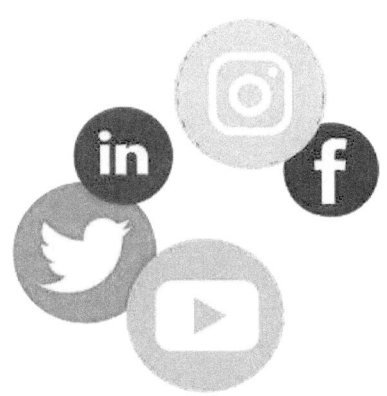

Health" (2017) have reached wide audiences, highlighting the health, environmental, and ethical reasons for adopting a vegan lifestyle.

Plant-Based Products: Over a last decade, the development of plant-based products like Beyond Meat and Impossible Foods has made veganism more accessible. The availability of vegan options in restaurants and grocery stores has significantly increased.

Health and Environmental Studies: Numerous studies have shown the health benefits of a vegan diet, including reduced risks of heart disease, diabetes, and certain cancers.

Additionally, research has highlighted the environmental benefits of reducing meat consumption, such as lowering greenhouse gas emissions and conserving resources.

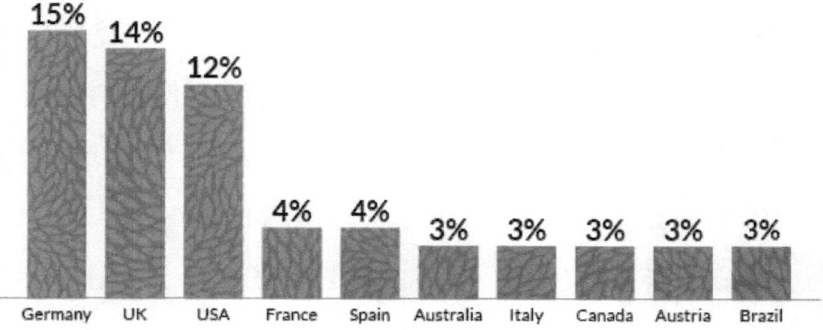

Global Movement and Worldwide Adoption

Vegan Population Growth:

The vegan population has grown significantly in countries like the United States, Canada, the United Kingdom, Australia, and parts of Europe and Asia. Institutional Support: Organizations such as the United Nations have recognized the benefits of plant-based diets for sustainability and food security.

Future Trends: Sustainability and Innovation: Technological Advances: Innovations in food technology, such as lab-grown meat and improved plant-based food production, continue to transform the vegan landscape.

Policy Changes: As veganism gains more mainstream acceptance, there may be significant policy changes to support plant-based diets and reduce reliance on animal agriculture.

Today various celebrities have embraced veganism, advocating for its ethical, health, and environmental benefits. Here are some prominent vegan celebrities

Joaquin Phoenix is a lifelong vegan and passionate animal rights activist. He has collaborated with organizations like PETA and narrated the documentary "Earthlings," which explores humanity's treatment of animals.

Natalie Portman has been a vocal advocate for veganism, producing and narrating the documentary "Eating Animals," which examines the impacts of factory farming. She frequently speaks about the ethical and environmental reasons for her vegan lifestyle.

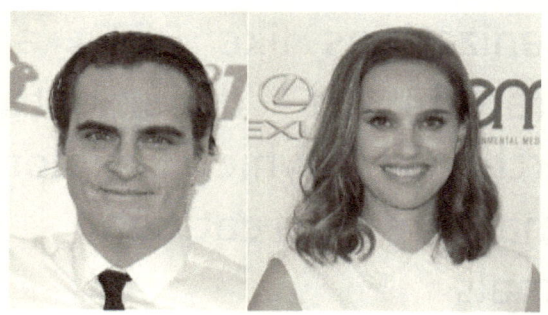

Miley Cyrus: She has been a vocal advocate for veganism, often sharing her views on animal rights and the benefits of a vegan lifestyle on social media. She has also been involved in various animal rescue initiative

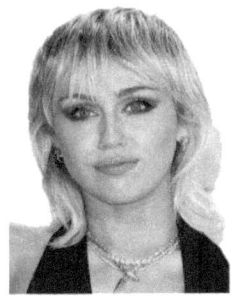 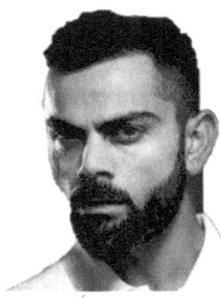 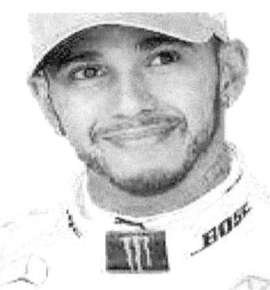

Virat Kohli: He turned vegetarian few years ago and relies only on vegan sources on a daily basis. He revealed that he quit non-vegetarian sources to add to his inspiring fitness level and it has helped him further.

Lewis Hamilton: He adopted a vegan lifestyle in 2017, motivated by concerns for his health, the environment, and animal welfare. Hamilton has been vocal about the benefits of a plant-based diet, crediting it for improved performance, better recovery times, and overall well-being.

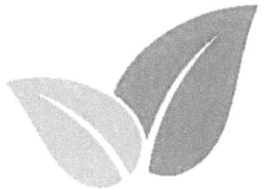

CHAPTER 3.
EARTH IN 21ST CENTURY:

In 21st century technology had growing like bubble. Every day, new technologies are emerging like AI, Solar Energy, Cyber security, etc. But with that environment is badly facing challenges such as:

Climate Change: The ongoing threat of climate change, with its associated extreme weather events and long-term impacts on ecosystems and human societies.

Resource **Depletion:** Over-extraction of natural resources, leading to depletion and environmental degradation.

Veganism is a powerful way to protect the Earth.

By adopting a plant-based diet, you can contribute to reducing greenhouse gas emissions, conserving water, preserving forests and habitats, reducing pollution, using land more efficiently, mitigating climate change, and promoting sustainable food systems. Every vegan choice helps create a healthier planet for future generations.

Reduced Greenhouse Gas Emissions:

Animal agriculture is a major contributor to greenhouse gas emissions, including methane and nitrous oxide. Choosing veganism helps reduce your carbon footprint significantly.

Major Greenhouse Gases

Carbon Dioxide (CO_2):
Sources: Fossil fuel combustion (coal, oil, natural gas), deforestation, and certain industrial processes.

Impact: The most significant GHG due to its high concentration and long atmospheric lifetime.

Methane (CH_4):
Sources: Agriculture (especially livestock digestion), landfills, oil and gas extraction, and wetlands.

Impact: Although present in smaller quantities than CO_2, methane is about 25 times more effective at trapping heat over a 100-year period.

Nitrous Oxide (N2O):

Sources: Agricultural activities (fertilizer application), industrial processes, and combustion of organic matter and fossil fuels.

Impact: Approximately 298 times more effective than CO2 at trapping heat over a 100- year period.

Fluorinated Gases:

Sources: Industrial processes, refrigerants, and manufacturing of some electrical components.

Impact: Varying global warming potentials (GWP), some thousands of times more potent than CO_2.

Hydrofluorocarbons (HFCs): Sources: Hydrofluorocarbons (HFCs), perfluorocarbons (PFCs), sulfur hexafluoride (SF6), and nitrogen trifluoride (NF3).

Impact: Varying global warming potentials (GWP), some thousands of times more potent than CO_2.

Greenhouse Effect:

The greenhouse effect is a natural process where certain gases in Earth's atmosphere trap heat from the sun, keeping the planet warm enough to support life. Human activities, particularly the burning of fossil fuels and deforestation, have intensified this effect by increasing the concentrations of these gases.

Measuring GHG Emissions CO2 Equivalent (CO2e):

Emissions of different GHGs are often expressed as CO_2 equivalents to account for their varying global warming potentials.

CO2 equivalents to account for their varying global warming potentials.

Sources of Emissions:

Energy Sector: Largest source, primarily from burning fossil fuels for electricity, heat, and transportation.

Agriculture: Methane from livestock and rice paddies, nitrous oxide from fertilized soils.

Industry: CO2 from cement production, CH4 from chemical production, and various fluorinated gases.

Waste: Methane from landfills and wastewater treatment.

Mitigation Strategies:
Energy Efficiency:

Improving the efficiency of buildings, vehicles, and appliances to reduce energy consumption.

Renewable Energy:

Increasing the use of wind, solar, hydro, and other renewable sources to replace fossil fuels.

Carbon Capture and Storage (CCS):

Capturing CO2 emissions at their source and storing them underground.

Afforestation and Reforestation:

Planting trees to absorb CO2 from the atmosphere.

Regulations and Policies:

Implementing policies to limit emissions, such as carbon pricing, emissions trading systems, and renewable energy mandates.

Conservation of Water Resources: Producing animal products requires large amounts of water.

A vegan diet uses significantly less water, contributing to the conservation of this vital resource.

Here are the key aspects of water conservation:

Sustainability: Ensures that water resources are available for future generations.

Environmental Protection: Maintains ecosystems and biodiversity that depend on water.

Economic Benefits: Reduces the costs associated with water treatment and supply.

Climate Change Mitigation: Helps manage the impacts of climate change, such as droughts and changing precipitation patterns.

Social Equity: Ensures that all communities have access to clean and safe water.

Water-efficient Fixtures:

Installing low-flow toilets, showerheads, and faucets to reduce water use.

Fixing Leaks: Repairing dripping faucets, pipes, and toilets to prevent water waste.

Smart Water Use: Using water-saving practices such as turning off the tap while brushing teeth and taking shorter showers.

Water-wise Landscaping:
Choosing drought- tolerant plants, using mulch, and employing efficient irrigation systems like drip irrigation.

Rainwater Harvesting:

Collecting and storing rainwater for use in irrigation and other non- potable purposes.

Agricultural Practices:

Efficient Irrigation Systems: Implementing drip irrigation, sprinklers, and scheduling irrigation to minimize water loss.

Soil Moisture Management: Using techniques like mulching and soil amendments to retain soil moisture.

Crop Selection: Growing crops suited to the local climate and water availability.

Conservation Tillage:

Reducing tillage to maintain soil structure and moisture.

Industrial and Commercial Practices:

Water Recycling and Reuse: Treating and reusing wastewater within industrial processes.

Water-efficient Technologies: Adopting equipment and processes that use less water.

Leak Detection and Repair: Regularly inspecting and maintaining infrastructure to prevent leaks.

Employee Training: Educating employees about water

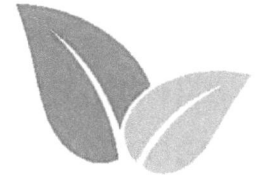

CHAPTER 4.
TO SAVE OUR PLANET:

Veganism can play a significant role in **saving Planet Earth** by addressing various environmental issues associated with animal agriculture. Here are the key ways veganism contributes to environmental sustainability:

Reducing Greenhouse Gas Emissions

Lower Emissions: Animal agriculture is responsible for a large portion of global greenhouse gas emissions, including methane from ruminant digestion and nitrous oxide from manure and fertilizers. A vegan diet reduces these emissions substantially.

Climate Change Mitigation: By decreasing the demand for animal products, veganism helps slow down the progression of climate change, which is crucial for maintaining global temperature rise within safe limits.

Conserving Water Resources:

Water Efficiency: Producing plant-based foods generally requires less water compared to raising animals for meat and dairy. For example, it takes about 1,800 gallons of water to produce a pound of beef, whereas many plant-based foods have a significantly lower water footprint.

Protecting Aquatic Ecosystems:

Reducing water usage helps maintain freshwater supplies and supports the health of aquatic ecosystems, which are often disrupted by water-intensive livestock farming.

Preserving Forests and Biodiversity

Forest Conservation: Large areas of forests, especially in the Amazon, are cleared for cattle grazing and growing feed crops. A shift towards veganism reduces the need for these practices, helping to preserve critical forest habitats.

Biodiversity Protection: Forests and other natural habitats are home to countless species. By preventing deforestation and habitat destruction, veganism aids in protecting biodiversity.

Reducing Pollution

Water Pollution: Runoff from livestock farms, including manure and fertilizers, often pollutes rivers, lakes, and oceans, leading to dead zones and harming aquatic life. A plant-based diet reduces this type of pollution.

Air Quality: Livestock farming releases pollutants such as ammonia and particulate matter into the air, which can harm human health and ecosystems.

Reducing livestock farming helps improve air quality.

Promoting Efficient Land Use

Land Efficiency: Producing plant-based foods typically requires less land than producing meat and dairy. For example, it takes far more land to raise cattle and grow their feed compared to growing crops directly for human consumption.

Reforestation and Rewilding: Land freed up from animal agriculture can be used for reforestation and rewilding projects, which can sequester carbon, restore ecosystems, and support wildlife.

Supporting Sustainable Agriculture

Reduced Resource Use: Plant-based diets generally use fewer natural resources (water, land, energy) compared to diets rich in animal products, making agriculture more sustainable.

Resilient Food Systems:

A shift towards plant- based agriculture can create more resilient food systems that are better equipped to withstand climate change and other environmental pressures.

Mitigating Climate Change

Carbon Sequestration:

By reducing deforestation and promoting reforestation, veganism aids in carbon sequestration, a natural process where trees and plants absorb carbon dioxide from the atmosphere.

Lower Carbon Footprint: Plant-based foods generally have a lower carbon footprint than animal products. By adopting a vegan diet, individuals can significantly reduce their personal carbon footprint.

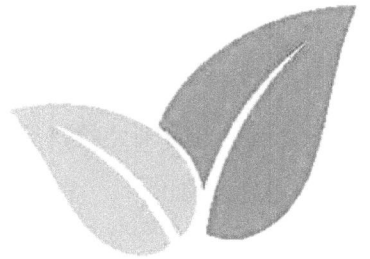

CHAPTER 5.
FOUNDATION OF VEGAN LIFESTYLE:

The history of veganism is a rich tapestry woven with threads of compassion, ethics, health, and environmental awareness. While the term "vegan" was coined relatively recently in the 20th century, the principles and practices of abstaining from animal products date back centuries.

Early Influences:
The roots of veganism can be traced back to ancient cultures and religious traditions that advocated for plant-based diets for ethical, spiritual, or health reasons. Philosophers and thinkers throughout history such as Pythagoras, Leonardo da Vinci,

and Mahatma Gandhi, espoused vegetarian diets and compassion for animals.

Emergence of Veganism:

Vegetarianism gained popularity in the 19th and early 20th Century as a response to concerns about animal welfare, health, and social justice. Vegetarian societies were formed in Europe and North America to promote plant-based diets and ethical living

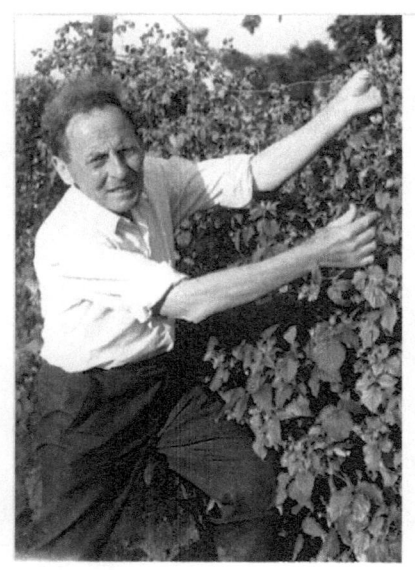 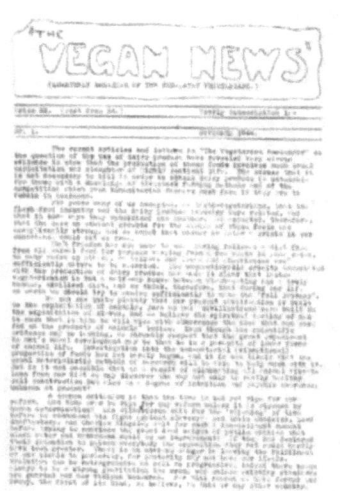

Founding of Veganism:

The term "vegan" was coined in 1944 by Donald Watson and his associates who founded the Vegan Society in the United Kingdom. They aimed to differentiate themselves from vegetarians who consumed dairy and eggs, advocating for a plant-based lifestyle free from all animal products.

The Vegan Society defined veganism as "a way of living that seeks to exclude, as far as possible and practicable, all forms of exploitation of, and cruelty to, animals for food, clothing, or any other purpose.

Early Vegan Advocacy:

In the **mid-20th** century, veganism gained traction as a social and ethical movement, with activists promoting the principles of vegan living through publications, lectures, and community organizing.

Prominent figures such as Frances Moore Lappé, Ruth Harrison, and Peter Singer contributed to the growing awareness of animal rights and veganism.

Mainstream Acceptance: Over the decades, veganism has become increasingly mainstream, with growing awareness of animal welfare issues, environmental degradation, and the health benefits of plant-based diets. Vegan alternatives to traditional animal products have become increasingly available and accessible, contributing to the mainstream acceptance of veganism.

Global Spread:

Veganism has spread globally, with individuals and communities around the world embracing plant-based diets and lifestyles as a means of promoting compassion, sustainability, and well-being for all beings. Vegan festivals, restaurants, and products have proliferated in many countries, reflecting the growing popularity and acceptance of veganism Worldwide.

Intersectionality and Social Justice: In recent years, veganism has intersected with broader social justice movements, including environmentalism, feminism, racial justice, and food sovereignty. Vegan activists increasingly advocate for a more inclusive and intersectional approach to veganism that addresses system inequalities and promotes social justice for humans and animals alike. my journey into veganism.

Overall, the history of veganism is a testament to the power of compassion, ethics, and activism in shaping our relationship with animals, the environment, and each other. As veganism continues to evolve, it serves as a beacon of hope for a more compassionate, sustainable, and just world for all beings

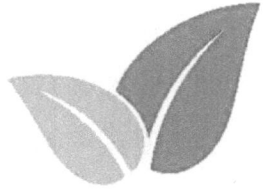

Chapter 6
ANIMAL CONSUMPTION:

Estimating the average amount of animal consumption by human beings per day involves looking at various types of animal products, including meat, dairy, and eggs. The amount can vary widely depending on dietary habits, cultural preferences, and economic factors across different regions. Here is a general overview based on global averages:

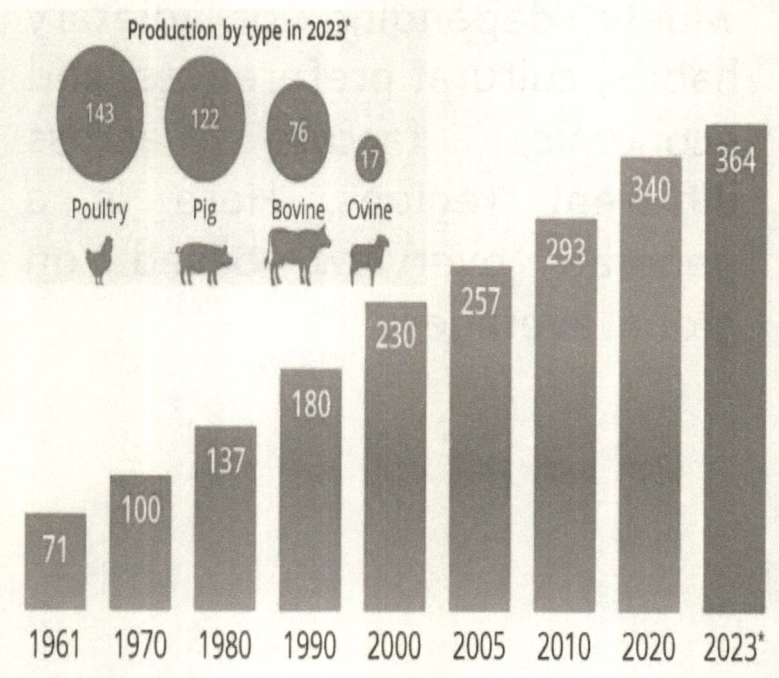

Global Averages of Animal Consumption Meat Consumption:

Per Capita Meat Consumption: According to the Food and Agriculture Organization (FAO), the global average per capita meat consumption is about 43 kg per year (as of recent data).

Daily Average: This translates to approximately 118 grams (0.26 pounds) of meat per person per day.

Dairy Consumption:

Per Capita Dairy Consumption:

The global average for dairy consumption is around 87 kg per year.

Daily Average: This equals about 238 grams (0.52 pounds) of dairy products per person per day, including milk, cheese, yogurt, etc.

Egg Consumption:

Per Capita Egg Consumption: On average, a person consumes about 9.1 kg of eggs per year.

Daily Average: This is approximately 25 grams (0.055 pounds) of eggs per person per day, roughly equivalent to half an egg.

Talking about India **Non - vegetarian** foods are increasingly becoming a part of the Indian platter as more people have begun relishing chicken, mutton, or fish in their meals. In the five years leading up to 2021, the prevalence of non-vegetarianism among women increased in 26 states/UTs, and in 25 states/UTs among men.

Women who included non-veg food in their meal at least once a week increased in Jharkhand by 16.4 percentage points; Telangana by 14.7

percentage points; Andhra Pradesh by 12.4 percentage points; and Bihar by 11.4 percentage points. Same for men rose in Sikkim by 27.7 percentage points; Maharashtra by 9.3 percentage points; Punjab by 8.9 percentage points; and Odisha by 7.3 percentage points.

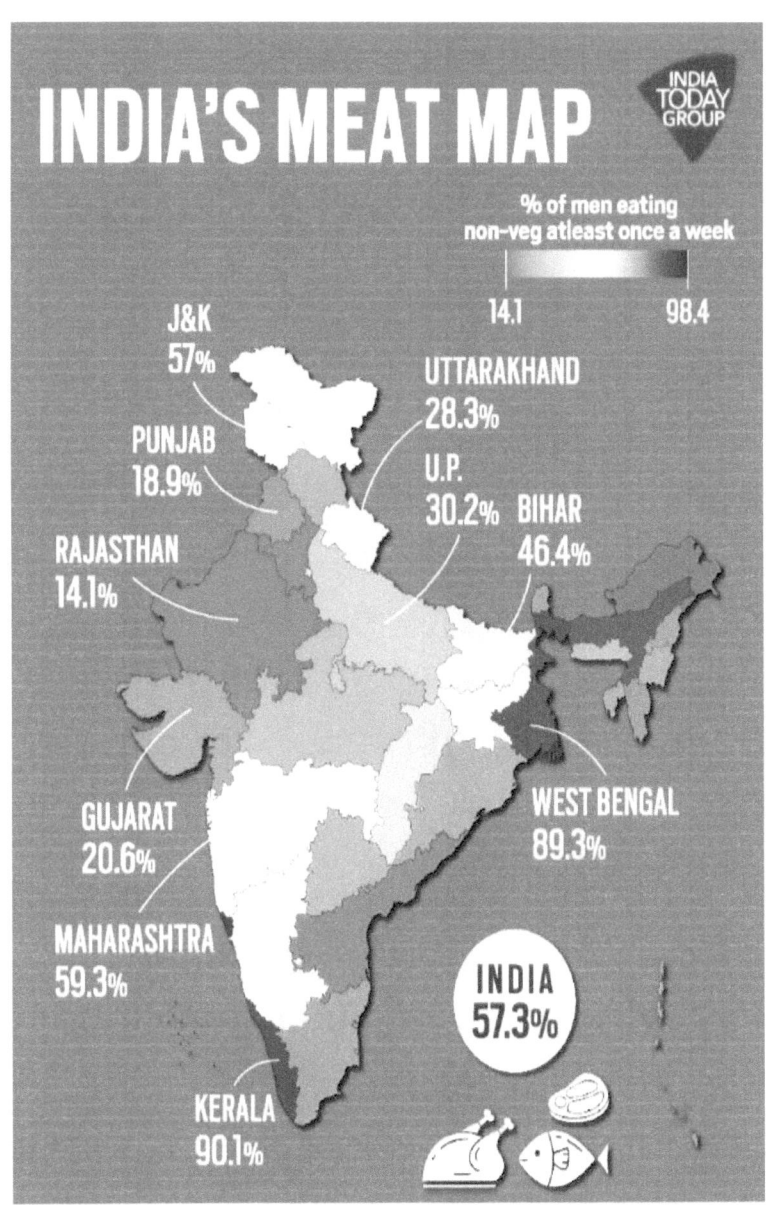

Regional Variations

These global averages can mask significant regional differences:

High Consumption Regions:

In countries like the United States, Australia, and much of Europe, meat consumption can be much higher. For example, the U.S. averages about 124 kg of meat per year per capita, or roughly 340 grams per day.

Low Consumption Regions:

In many parts of Asia, Africa, and some areas of South

America, meat consumption is much lower due to economic, cultural, or religious reasons. Some countries may average only 20-30 kg per year, or around 55-82 grams per day.

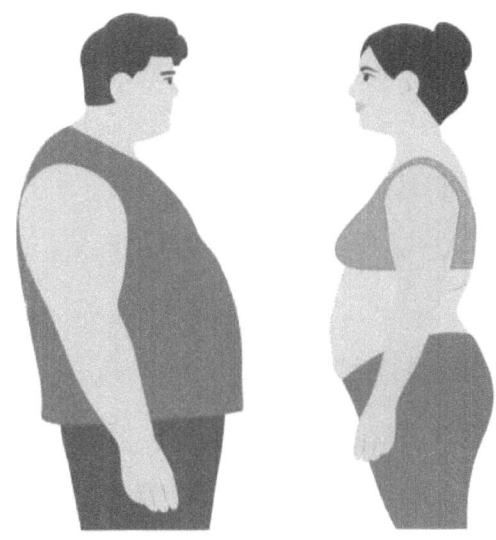

Health and Sustainability Considerations

The consumption levels of animal products have significant health and environmental implications:

Health Impact: High consumption of red and processed meats is linked to various health issues, including heart disease, certain cancers, and diabetes. Balanced consumption with more plant-based foods is recommended for better health outcomes.

Environmental Impact: Meat production is resource-intensive, requiring large amounts of water, feed, and land, and it is a major contributor to greenhouse gas emissions. Reducing meat consumption and shifting towards plant-based diets are often suggested to lessen environmental impact.

CHAPTER 7.
IMPACT OF VEGANISM ON EARTH:

Exploring the ethical, environmental, and health reasons for adopting a vegan lifestyle.

Addressing common misconceptions and myths surrounding veganism.

Veganism offers several environmental benefits that stem from the reduction or elimination of animal agriculture and the consumption of animal products. Here are some key environmental advantages of adopting a vegan lifestyle:

Reduced Greenhouse Gas Emissions:

Animal agriculture is a significant contributor to greenhouse gas emissions, particularly methane and nitrous oxide. By eliminating or reducing animal products from one's diet, individuals can lower their carbon footprint, mitigating climate change impacts.

Conservation of Natural Resources:

Animal agriculture requires vast amounts of land, water, and energy. Producing plant-based foods generally require fewer resources compared to raising livestock for meat, dairy, and eggs. By choosing plant-based options, Individuals can help conserve land, water, and energy resources.

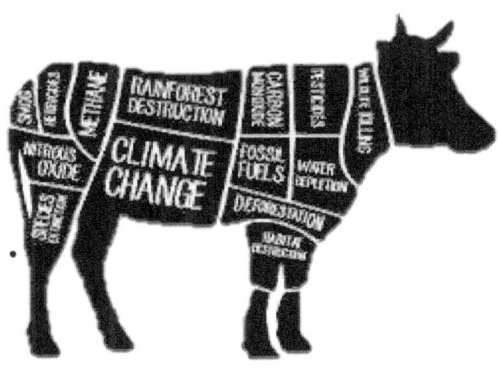

Preservation of Biodiversity:

Livestock farming often involves deforestation and habitat destruction to create grazing land and grow feed crops. By reducing the demand for animal products, veganism helps protect natural habitats and preserves biodiversity, safeguarding ecosystems and wildlife.

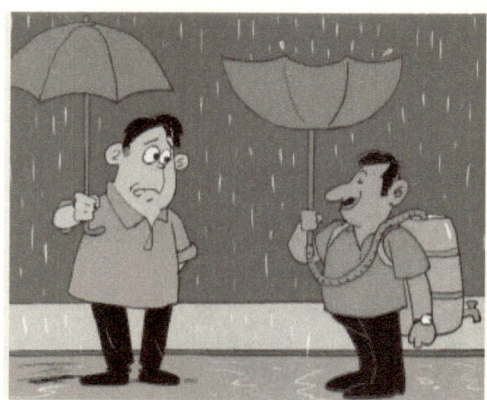

Water Conservation:

Animal agriculture is water intensive, requiring large quantities of water for drinking, cleaning, and irrigation of feed crops. By opting for plant-based foods,

individuals can significantly reduce their water footprint, as plant-based agriculture generally requires less water compared to raising animals for food.

Reduction of Pollution:

Animal agriculture contributes to various forms of environmental pollution, including water pollution from runoff of animal waste and chemicals used in farming, air pollution from methane emissions, and soil degradation from overgrazing. Veganism can help mitigate these forms of pollution by reducing the demand for animal farming practices.

Mitigation of Deforestation:

Livestock farming is a leading cause of deforestation, particularly in regions like the Amazon rainforest where vast areas are cleared for cattle ranching and soy cultivation for animal feed. Choosing plant based foods can help reduce the demand for products linked to deforestation, thus contributing to forest conservation efforts.

Overall, veganism offers a sustainable dietary choice that aligns with efforts to address pressing environmental challenges such as climate change, resource depletion, biodiversity loss, and pollution. By embracing plant-based diets, individuals can play a significant role in promoting a more environmentally sustainable future.

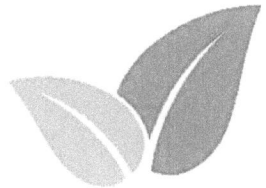

CHAPTER 8.

DEBUNKING MYTHS:

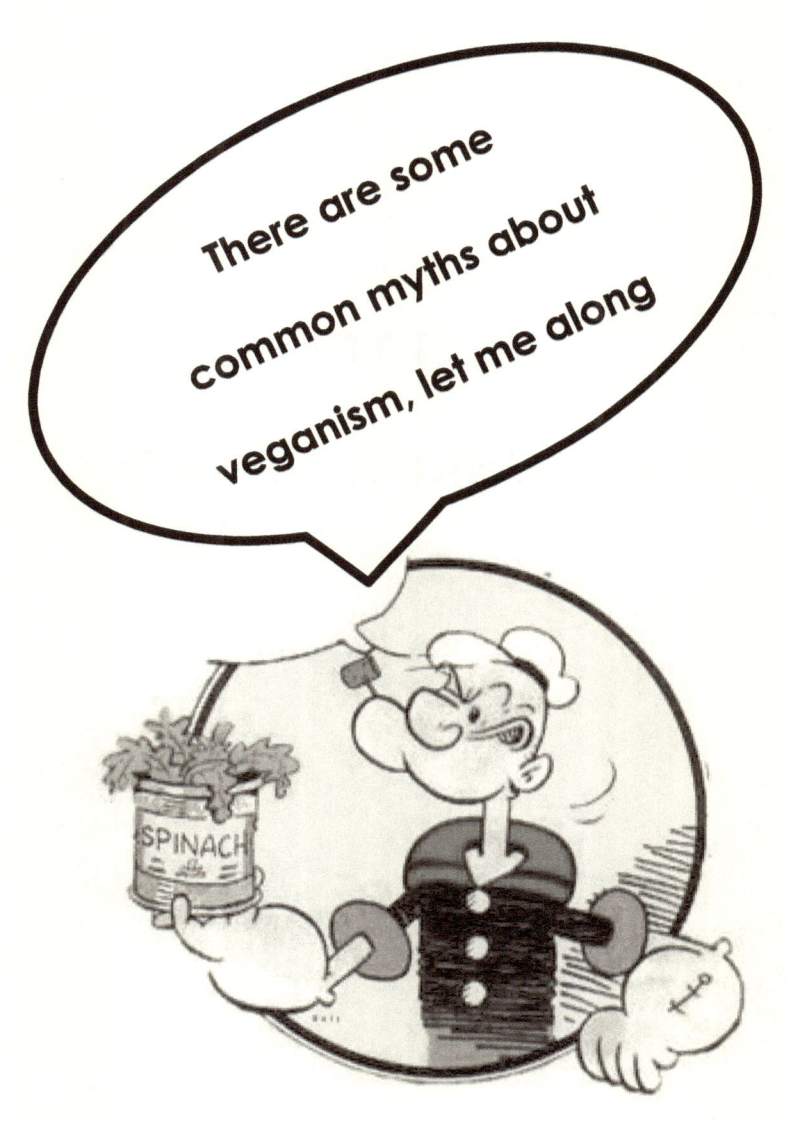

Myth:

Vegan diets lack protein.

Fact:

Plant-based diets can provide more than enough protein when a variety of plant foods such as legumes, tofu, tempeh, seitan, nuts, seeds, and grains are consumed. Adequate protein intake is easily achievable on a well-planned vegan diet.

Myth:

Vegan diets are deficient in essential nutrients.

Fact:

With proper planning, vegan diets can be nutritionally adequate and provide all essential nutrients. Key nutrients like protein, iron, calcium, vitamin D, vitamin B12, omega-3 fatty acids, and zinc can be obtained from a variety of plant-based sources and fortified foods or supplements.

Myth:
Vegan diets are expensive.

Fact:
Vegan diets can be affordable and cost effective, especially when based on whole plant foods such as grains, legumes, fruits, vegetables, nuts, and seeds. Staples like beans, rice, pasta, and seasonal produce are often budget friendly options.

Myth:

Vegan diets are restrictive and boring.

Fact:
Vegan diets offer a wide variety of delicious and satisfying foods, including fruits, vegetables, grains, legumes, nuts, seeds, herbs, spices, and plant-based meat and dairy alternatives. With creativity and culinary exploration, vegan meals can be flavorful, diverse, and enjoyable.

Myth:

Veganism is only about diet.

Fact:

While diet is a central aspect of veganism, it extends beyond food choices to encompass a lifestyle that seeks to minimize harm to animals in all

aspects.

Myth:

Vegans don't get enough protein:

Fact:

One of the most pervasive myths about veganism is that it's difficult to get enough protein on a plant-based diet. In reality, there are plenty of plant-based sources of protein such as beans, lentils, tofu, tempeh, seitan, quinoa, nuts, and seeds. With proper meal planning, vegans can easily meet their protein needs.

Myth:

Vegan diets are restrictive and boring:

Fact:

Many people believe that vegan diets are limited and lack variety, leading to bland and boring meals. In reality, vegan cuisine is incredibly diverse and creative, with a wide range of delicious dishes from around the world. With endless possibilities for plant-based ingredients and flavors, vegan cooking can be exciting, flavorful, and satisfying.

Overall, these myths about veganism are based on misconceptions and misinformation. By dispelling these myths and providing accurate

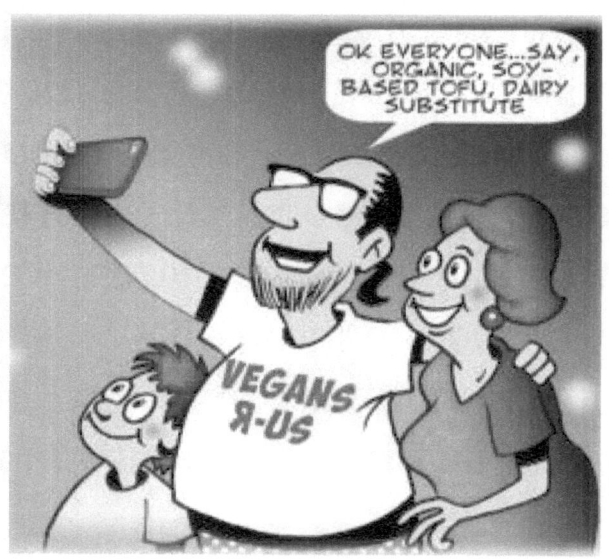

information about vegan diets, we can promote a better understanding of plant-based living and encourage more people to embrace compassionate, sustainable, and healthy food choices.

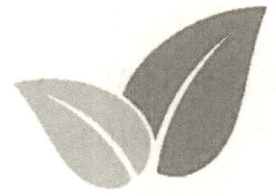

CHAPTER 9.

HEALTH BENEFITS OF VEGAN PLATE:

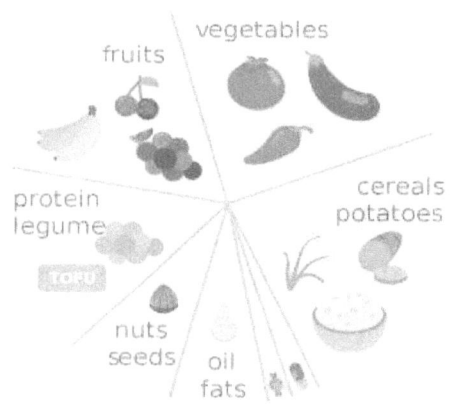

A vegan diet, which excludes all animal products including meat, dairy, eggs, and sometimes honey, can offer numerous health benefits:

Lower risk of chronic diseases:

Studies suggest that a vegan diet can lower the risk of heart disease, hypertension, type 2 diabetes, certain cancers, and obesity. This is often attributed to the higher intake of fruits, vegetables, whole grains, nuts, and seeds, which are rich in vitamins, minerals, antioxidants, and fiber.

Heart health:

Vegan diets are typically low in saturated fats and cholesterol, which are commonly found in animal products. High intake of fruits, vegetables, and plant-based fats can help reduce blood pressure and cholesterol levels, thereby improving heart health.

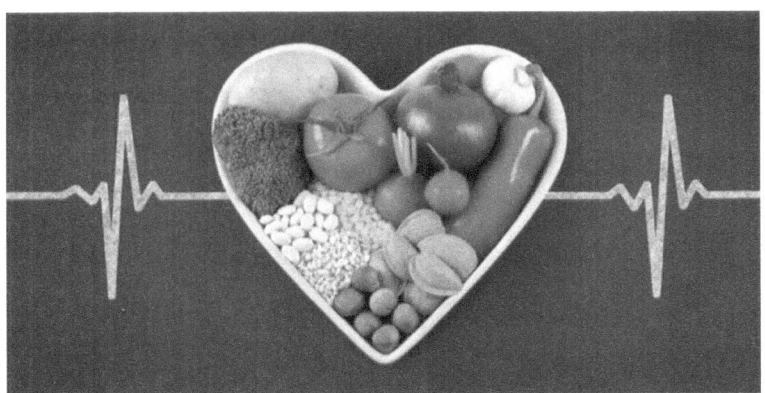

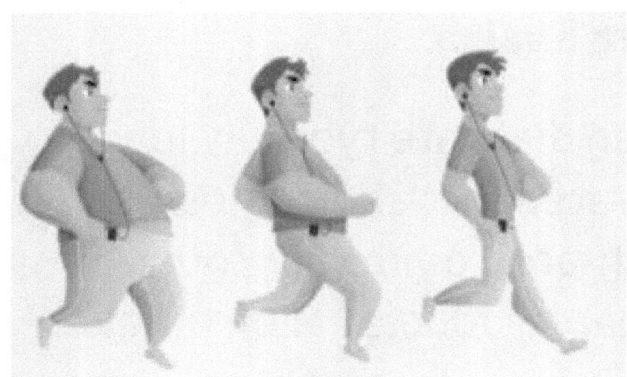

Weight management:

Vegan diets tend to be lower in calories and saturated fats while being higher in fiber, which can aid in weight loss or weight management.

Plant-based diets are associated with lower body mass-index (BMI) and reduced risk of obesity.

Improved digestion:

Plant-based diets are rich in fiber, which can promote healthy digestion and prevent constipation. Increased fiber intake can also support a diverse and healthy gut microbiome, which is essential for overall health.

Lower risk of certain cancers:

Some studies suggest that a vegan diet may lower the risk of certain types of cancer, particularly colorectal cancer.

The high intake of fruits, vegetables, and fiber, along with the absence of processed and red meats, may contribute to this protective effect.

Better blood sugar control:

Vegan diets can improve insulin sensitivity and glycemic control, making them beneficial for individuals with type 2 diabetes or those at risk of developing diabetes. Plant-based foods have a lower glycemic index and may help stabilize blood sugar levels.

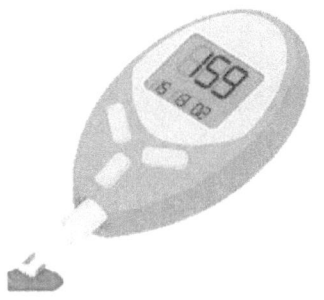

Reduced inflammation:

Plant-based diets are naturally anti-inflammatory due to the abundance of antioxidants and phytonutrients found in fruits, vegetables, and other plant foods. Lowering inflammation in the body can help reduce the risk of chronic diseases and promote overall well-being.

Improved nutrient intake:

While it's essential for vegans to pay attention to certain nutrients like vitamin B12, iron, calcium, omega-3 fatty acids, and vitamin D, a well- planned vegan diet can provide all the necessary nutrients for optimal health. Many plant-based foods are rich sources of vitamins, minerals, and other beneficial compounds.

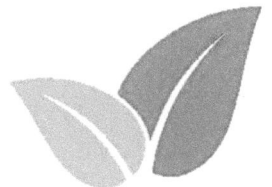

CHAPTER 10
PRACTICAL TIPS FOR VEGAN LIVING:

Here we will discuss some practical tips for Vegan living:

✓ **Grocery Shopping:** Tips for navigating the grocery store and stocking up on

vegan essentials.
- ✓ **Meal Planning:** Strategies for meal planning and prepping nutritious, delicious vegan meals.

- ✓ **Eating Out:** How to dine out as a vegan, including navigating restaurant menus and making special requests.
- ✓ **Vegan Cooking:** Beginner-friendly vegan recipes and cooking tips for creating flavorful plant-based dishes at home.
- ✓ **Supplementation:** Guidance on vegan supplements, including vitamin B12, vitamin D, omega-3 fatty

acids, and more.

Vegan Supplements:

Here are some common vegan supplements that individuals may consider incorporating into their diet:

Vitamin B12:

Vitamin B12 is essential for nerve function, DNA synthesis, and the production of red blood cells. Since it is primarily found in animal products, vegans may need to supplement with vitamin B12 to ensure adequate intake. Look for methyl cobalamin or cyanocobalamin supplements, and aim for a daily intake of 250- 500 mcg or follow your healthcare provider's recommendations.

Vitamin D:

Vitamin D plays a crucial role in bone health, immune function, and mood regulation. While sunlight exposure can stimulate vitamin D. synthesis in the skin, many people, including vegans, may benefit from supplementation, especially in regions with limited sunlight. Look for vegan vitamin D3 supplements derived from lichen or opt for vitamin D2 supplements. Aim for a daily intake of 600-800 IU or follow your healthcare provider's recommendations.

Omega-3 Fatty Acids:

Omega-3 fatty acids, particularly EPA and DHA, are essential for heart health, brain function, and inflammation regulation. While fatty fish is a common source of EPA and DHA, vegans can obtain these nutrients from algae- based supplements. Look for supplements that provide both EPA and DHA, and aim for a daily intake of 200-300 mg combined EPA and DHA or follow your healthcare provider's recommendations.

Calcium:

Calcium is essential for bone health, muscle function, and nerve transmission. While dairy products are a common source of calcium, vegans can obtain this mineral from fortified plant-based foods like fortified plant milks, tofu, tempeh, and leafy greens. If your calcium intake from food is inadequate, consider supplementing with calcium carbonate or calcium citrate. Aim for a daily intake of 1000-1200 mg or follow your healthcare provider's recommendations.

Iron:

Iron is vital for oxygen transport, energy production, and immune function. While plant-based sources like legumes, tofu, seeds, and leafy greens provide iron, the absorption of non-heme iron from plant foods may be lower than heme iron from animal products. To enhance iron absorption, consume vitamin C-rich foods.

alongside iron-rich foods and consider taking an iron supplement if your iron levels are low. Aim for a daily intake of 18 mg for adult women and 8 mg for adult men or follow your healthcare provider's recommendations.

Zinc:

Zinc is involved in immune function, wound healing, and DNA synthesis. While zinc is present in plant foods like legumes, nuts, seeds, and whole grains, phytates in plant foods can inhibit its absorption.

Consider supplementing with zinc if your intake is inadequate or if you have increased zinc needs due to factors like pregnancy or intense physical activity. Aim for a daily intake of 8-11 mg for adults or follow your healthcare provider's recommendations.

Before starting any supplement regimen, it's essential to consult with a healthcare provider or registered dietitian to determine **your individual nutrient needs** and ensure that supplements are appropriate for you.

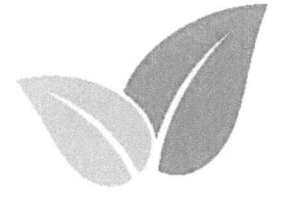

CHAPTER 11.

VEGAN DAIRY:

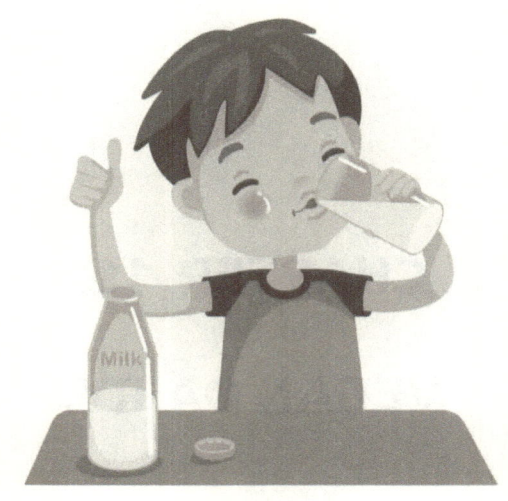

Milk and milk products are preferred as our daily need.

But, we have many healthy vegan dairy products to eat.

These dairy products are plant-based alternatives to traditional dairy products that do not involve any animal-derived ingredients.

They are made from various plant sources such as nuts, seeds, grains, and legumes.

Here are some popular vegan dairy products:

- ✓ **Almond Milk:** Made from almonds, it has a mild, nutty flavor and is often fortified with vitamins and minerals.
- ✓ **Soy Milk:** Made from soybeans, it is high in protein and often enriched with calcium and vitamins.
- ✓ **Oat Milk:** Made from oats, it has a creamy texture and is a good source of fiber.
- ✓ **Coconut Milk:** Made from the flesh of coconuts, it

has a rich, creamy texture and a slight coconut flavor.
- ✓ **Rice Milk:** Made from milled rice and water, it has a thin consistency and a naturally sweet flavor.
- ✓ **Cashew Milk:** Made from cashews, it has a creamy texture and a slightly sweet, nutty flavor.
- ✓ **Hemp Milk:** Made from hemp seeds, it is a good source of omega-3 and omega-6 fatty acids.

Vegan Cheese Alternatives

- **Nut-Based Cheeses:** Made from nuts like cashews, almonds, and macadamias, they can be cultured and aged to mimic traditional cheeses.
- **Soy-Based Cheeses:** Made from soy protein, they come in various forms like slices, shreds, and blocks.
- **Coconut-Based Cheeses:** Made from coconut oil and other plant-based ingredients, often fortified with nutritional yeast for a cheesy flavor.
- **Potato and Carrot-Based**

- ✓ **Cheeses:** Made from vegetables, often used in homemade cheese sauces.

Vegan Yogurt Alternatives

- ✓ **Soy Yogurt:** Made from soy milk, available in various flavors and often enriched with probiotics.
- ✓ **Coconut Yogurt:** Made from coconut milk, it has a rich and creamy texture, available in plain and flavored varieties.
- ✓ **Almond Yogurt:** Made from almond milk, it is often fortified with probiotics and comes in various flavors.

✓ **Oat Yogurt:** Made from oat milk, it is creamy and can be found in plain and flavored options.

Vegan Butter Alternatives

✓ **Margarine:** Look for brands that specifically state they are vegan, as some margarine may contain dairy derivatives.
✓ **Nut and Seed Butters:** Such as almond butter, peanut butter, and sunflower seed butter, often used as spreads.
✓ **Coconut Oil:** Used as a butter substitute in baking and

- cooking.

Vegan Cream Alternatives

- **Coconut Cream:** Made from coconut milk, it is thick and can be used in desserts and cooking.
- **Cashew Cream:** Made from blended cashews, it can be used as a base for sauces and soups.
- **Soy Cream:** Made from soy milk, it can be used as a substitute for dairy cream in cooking and baking.

Vegan Ice Cream Alternatives

- **Coconut Milk Ice Cream:** Made from coconut milk, it is rich and creamy, available in many flavors.
- **Almond Milk Ice Cream:** Made from almond milk, it is lighter and available in various flavors.
- **Soy Milk Ice Cream:** Made from soy milk, it is high in protein and available in many varieties.
- **Cashew Milk Ice Cream:** Made from cashew milk, it is creamy and available in different flavors.

Vegan Sour Cream and Cream Cheese Alternatives

- ✓ **Cashew Sour Cream:** Made from blended cashews, it can be used as a substitute in recipes calling for sour cream.
- ✓ **Soy-Based Cream Cheese:** Made from soy milk, it comes in plain and flavored varieties.
- ✓ **Coconut-Based Cream Cheese:** Made from coconut milk, it is creamy and can be used as a spread.

Overall, our journey as a vegan and entrepreneur is driven by compassion, purpose, and a commitment to creating a better future for all beings.

You can contribute by sharing pdf of this book and purchase its hard copy online to help us.

www.ingramcontent.com/pod-product-compliance
Lightning Source LLC
Chambersburg PA
CBHW020431220526
45464CB00002B/657